A Look at
CUBISM

Written by
Sneed B. Collard III

rourkeeducationalmedia.com

www.rourkeeducationalmedia.com

PHOTO CREDITS: Cover, page 8, 11, 13, 15: © The Gallery Collection; page 1, 6: © Christie's Images; page 4, 5: © CynthiaAnnF; page 7, 18: © Associated Press, © adoc-photos; page 12: © Alinari Archives; page 14: © Wikipaintings - Bibemus Quarry; page 17: © Corbis; page 19: © Bettmann; page 20, 21: © Paul White/AP/Corbis; page 22: © mediaphotos

Edited by Precious McKenzie

Cover and Interior design by Tara Raymo

Library of Congress PCN Data

A Look at Cubism / Sneed B. Collard III
 (Art and Music)
  ISBN 978-1-62169-873-9 (hard cover)
  ISBN 978-1-62169-768-8 (soft cover)
  ISBN 978-1-62169-973-6 (e-Book)
Library of Congress Control Number: 2013936782

Rourke Educational Media
Printed in the United States of America,
North Mankato, Minnesota

Also Available as:

rourkeeducationalmedia.com

customerservice@rourkeeducationalmedia.com • PO Box 643328 Vero Beach, Florida 32964

Table of Contents

Chopping Things Up

Imagine taking four photographs of your school, each from a different side. You cut up the photographs and choose a few pieces from each one. Then you try to arrange the pieces into a new picture.

What would your new picture look like? Would you still recognize your school? What would it tell you about the world? These are the kinds of questions that led to a new kind of art called **Cubism**.

Artists for a Changing World

Bottle and Clarinet *by Georges Braque, 1911*

Two **artists** invented Cubism. Their names are Pablo Picasso and Georges Braque. They began painting in the late 1800s. Until this time, artists had tried to copy the world around them. They tried to draw and paint people and things as we all saw them.

Pablo Picasso
(1881-1973)

Pablo Picasso was born on October 25, 1881, in Spain. His father was a painter and an art teacher. It's no surprise that Picasso displayed an artistic talent at an early age.

Georges Braque
(1882-1963)

Georges Braque was born on May 13, 1882, in France. His father was a house painter and decorator. Braque learned many new skills from him that he later used in his art.

Woman Playing a Guitar by Georges Braque, 1913

But the world was changing rapidly. Factories were replacing farms. New scientific discoveries shifted the way people viewed the world. Picasso and Braque wanted to create a new kind of art. They wanted art that fit in better with the new world around them.

They realized that we don't look at the world from one fixed point. Our view of people and things is always changing. They asked themselves, how can we paint this changing viewpoint?

More Than a Pretty Picture

One way was to paint an object from several **angles**. For example, some parts of a person might be viewed from the right side. Other parts might be viewed from the left. Arms, legs, eyes, and mouth could be moved into different, unusual positions.

The viewers might still recognize the picture as a person. But now, they weren't just enjoying a pretty picture. They began asking questions about how they looked at the world.

The 1923 painting, The Bird Cage, *is one of*
Pablo Picasso's most well known paintings.

Before the Cubist movement, the most important thing in art was the **subject**, what a painting or **sculpture** was about. Now, the art itself became important.

Picasso and Braque did not invent the name Cubism. The name came from the many **geometric shapes** the artists used in their work. Picasso and Braque painted their first Cubist paintings in 1907 and 1908.

Houses at Estaque *by Georges Braque, 1908*

Some people loved the new approach. Others hated it. One thing was certain, Cubism turned the art world upside down!

Exploration

The art of Picasso and Braque changed as rapidly as the world around them. Their paintings became more **abstract**. This meant that subjects became harder and harder to recognize.

Bibemus Quarry *by Paul Cezanne, 1900*

Cubism was the first major abstract art form. Picasso and Braque, though, were influenced by many earlier artists. These included French artists Paul Gauguin and Paul Cezanne, as well as traditional African wood-carvers.

Mediterranean Landscape *by Pablo Picasso, 1952*

15

Picasso and Braque also began gluing paper, printed words, cloth, and other materials onto their paintings. These kinds of paintings were called **papiers collés**.

Papiers collés is a type of collage. Prior to Cubism, collage was not an accepted artistic practice. Artists may use newspaper clippings, photographs, ribbons, wood, and even portions of other artworks in their collages.

Abstract Art Gets Big

Alexander Archipenko (1887-1964) analyzed human figure and turned them into geometric forms. Walking Woman *is a bronze sculpture of a woman, approximately 2 feet (61 centimeters) high, in a walking pose, created in 1912.*

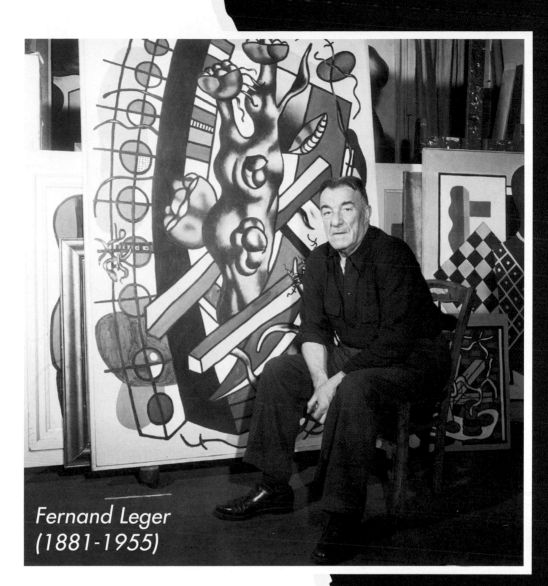

*Fernand Leger
(1881-1955)*

Fernand Leger was one of many artists who painted in a Cubist style. He often painted cylinders or tubes. This led some people to call his style "tubist"!

As Picasso and Braque became more successful, other artists also began making abstract art. Many artists did Cubist painting or sculpture. Others took abstract art in different, new directions.

Two Artists, Two Lives

As Braque grew older, he moved away from Cubism, but Picasso kept going back to it during his long life. Picasso's most famous Cubist work was a 25-foot long (762 centimeter) painting called *Guernica*. In the painting, Picasso used scary images to show the horrors of warfare.

Guernica by Pablo Picasso, 1937

Guernica is a small town in Spain. It was bombed by German planes in 1937 during Spain's civil war. Most of the victims were ordinary men, women, and children. Picasso's painting still stands as a protest against war and violence.

Leaving a Different World

Today, millions of artists still study the Cubist paintings and sculptures of these two men. Picasso and Braque did more than invent a new kind of art. They continue to stretch our imaginations.

"All children are artists. The problem is how to remain an artist once he grows up." Pablo Picasso

Glossary

abstract (ab-STRAKT): art that does not show things as they are in the real world, but uses colors and shapes to get a response from the viewer

angles (ANG-uhlz): the figures formed when two lines meet at the same point

artists (AHR-tists): people who are skilled at painting or making things

Cubism (KYOOB-iz-um): a style of art that uses geometric shapes to show many sides of something all at once

geometric shapes (jee-uh-MET-rik shayps): the outline of a form, such as a circle, square, rectangle, or triangle

papiers collés (pa-pyay kol-AY): paintings that have paper, cloth, and other objects attached to them

sculpture (SKUHLP-chur): an object that stands as a work of art, often carved or shaped from a hard material

subject (SUB-jekt): what a painting is about

Index

Websites

www.pablopicasso.org/index.jsp

www.georgesbraque.org/

www.metmuseum.org/toah/hd/cube/hd_cube.htm

About the Author

Sneed B. Collard III has written more than 65 books for young people including the award-winning books *Animal Dads, Shep: Our Most Loyal Dog, and Teeth*. Sneed has a special interest in history. His popular mysteries *The Governor's Dog is Missing* and *Hangman's Gold* feature history of the Old West, including famed Western artist Charles Russell. Watch book trailers for Sneed's books and learn more about him at www.sneedbcollardiii.com.

Meet The Author!
www.meetREMauthors.com